A Touch of His Power

Other Books in This Series

Meditations on God's Awesome Power

A Touch of His Power

with Original Photographs by

Charles Stanley

Zondervan Publishing House
Grand Rapids, Michigan

A Division of HarperCollins*Publishers*

A Touch of His Power
Copyright © 1999 by Charles F. Stanley

Requests for information should be addressed to:

📖 ZondervanPublishingHouse
Grand Rapids, Michigan 49530

Library of Congress Cataloging-in-Publication Data

Stanley, Charles F.
    A touch of his power : meditations on God's awesome power, with original photographs / by Charles Stanley.
      p.   cm.
    ISBN: 0-310-21492-0
      1. God Meditations. 2. Power (Christian theology) Meditations.
    I. Title.
    BT102.S67 1999
    231' .4--dc21   99-31729
                                                                          CIP

This edition printed on acid-free paper.

Interior design by Sherri L. Hoffman

Printed in the United States of America

99 00 01 02 03 04 /❖ DC/ 10 9 8 7 6 5 4 3 2

*To the Staff of In Touch Ministries whose
faithful and diligent labor continues to
help us touch the world with
the Word of God.*

Contents

$\mathcal{P}$hotographs

———— ◉ ————

Acknowledgments

I want to express my appreciation to Jim Dailey for his editorial assistance and to Tom Rogeberg for assisting me while photographing these scenes in Switzerland.

$\mathcal{I}$ntroduction

―――――――― ✦ ――――――――

$\mathcal{P}$ower is a hot commodity these days. Nations strive for it, businesses compete fiercely for it, and individuals can't get enough of it.

Perhaps the quest for power has accelerated in this age of global competition, but I believe we invest incredible effort to attain power for reasons that haven't changed throughout the millenniums. We like the perks of power—authority, prestige, influence, and security.

There is one significant problem. The Bible says that all power belongs exclusively to God. "In [God's] hands are strength and power to exalt and give strength to all" (1 Chronicles 29:12). Although the Scriptural words for "strength" and "power" do differ slightly, they are often used interchangeably and the ability, might, and authority they connote come from the Lord. God gives strength. God bestows power. The power that is enduring and used for the right purposes isn't conferred by men or women, money, or marketplace. God alone exercises sovereign power over nations and people. He is the source of all strength.

Thankfully, God is willing to give those of us who know and worship him a touch of his power. We cannot demand it or earn it. His power is a gift, and all we can do is humbly receive it. God delights in imparting his power to those who meet the one paradoxical requirement—weakness. The prophet Isaiah worded it magnificently: "He gives strength to the weary and increases the power of the weak. Even . . . young men stumble and fall; but those who hope in the LORD will renew their strength. They will soar on wings like eagles; they will run and not grow weary, they will walk and not be faint" (Isaiah 40:29–31).

If you need God's power, but feel hopelessly inadequate and undeserving, take courage—you are the person whom God will empower. If you have reached a place of exhaustion and emptiness, then look ever so faintly to the heavens and let God breathe his power into your spirit. Those who are brokenhearted and at the very end of their own resources are but a heart's cry away from the renewing surge of Christ's sustaining power. God gives his power to the humble and wanting, not for the advancement of personal interests and agenda, but for honoring his name. The power of Christ is not for clout, but for service; not for self-gratification, but for the glorification of Christ. He strengthens us that we might demonstrate to others his sufficiency. God uses the humble, feeble efforts of Christian men and women to display his supremacy.

The apostle Paul is renowned for his premier role in spreading the gospel. He confronted opposition and obstacles at almost every turn, which only served to propel him to further resolve and commitment. "Therefore I will boast all the more gladly about my weaknesses, so that Christ's power may rest on me" (2 Corinthians 12:9).

A Touch of His Power is for those people who, like Paul, are acutely aware of their personal weaknesses. If you are weary and troubled, read on—for you are the very person whom God stands ready to strengthen.

A Touch of His Power

I am still as strong today as the day Moses sent me out;
I'm just as vigorous to go out to battle now as I was then.

JOSHUA 14:11

Go in God's Strength

---●---

Tackling the strife in our lives is such a wearisome task that we often take the easier route of retreat and escape. We grow weary of fighting giants.

At times like this we can find inspiration by reading the story of Caleb, who at an advanced age was still eager to confront imposing obstacles. At the young and robust age of forty, Caleb had been chosen by Moses to be one of twelve spies to check out Canaan. You know the story. Only Caleb and Joshua reported back with a victor's perspective.

Forty-five years later, Caleb was finally in the Promised Land, and he still had plenty of spunk. As Joshua divided the land to the Hebrew tribes, Caleb already knew what he wanted. "Now give me this hill country that the LORD promised me that day. You yourself heard then that the Anakites [giants] were there and their cities were large and fortified, but, the LORD helping me, I will drive them out just as he said" (Joshua 14:12).

Caleb had spent over forty years in the hot, dry wilderness. He had spent several years fighting alongside Joshua in Canaan. Wasn't that enough arduous times for a man his age? Why not settle down in a broad valley and take it easy? Instead, Caleb was ready for more conquests, even if it meant taking rugged terrain occupied by fierce, gigantic enemies.

Caleb obviously was gifted with robust physical strength from the Lord, but his real secret was in his heart. Caleb "followed the LORD wholeheartedly" (14:8, 14). When our hearts are set on following hard after Christ, we can overcome personal weaknesses and difficult circumstances.

That means looking at our odds through the eyes of faith. Caleb saw the power of God, not the size of his adversary. Giants *are* big. Anger *is* huge. Greed *is* enormous. Pride *is* gargantuan. These things are more powerful than we are, but God is greater still. God slays the giants that inhabit our spiritual landscape; if we keep looking to him and not ourselves, we can win by his strength. As Jehoshaphat cried out when he was surrounded by invading armies, "We have no power to face this vast army that is attacking us. We do not know what to do, but our eyes are upon you" (2 Chronicles 20:12).

If you are flagging or failing in your battles against great odds, you can find the strength you need by looking to the great power of God. The heart fully devoted to Christ trusts fully in him. "For the eyes of the LORD range throughout the earth to strengthen those whose hearts are fully committed to him" (2 Chronicles 16:9).

———— • ————

Father, right now, I give to you _____.
Forgive me for holding on to it and trying to tackle it in my own strength. I give it to you, and I trust you for the outcome.

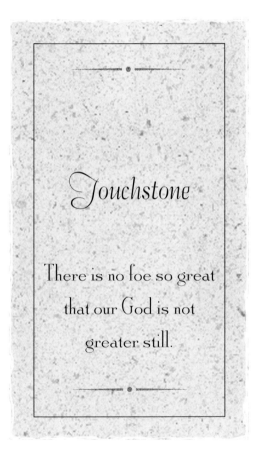

Touchstone

There is no foe so great
that our God is not
greater still.

Your strength will equal your days.

DEUTERONOMY 33:25

Strength Through Contentment

—————— ⬢ ——————

While working in his garden one day, Saint Augustine was asked what he would do if he knew that Christ would return that evening. Augustine stopped for a moment, leaned against his hoe, and replied, "I would keep hoeing my garden."

Great strength comes from a contented spirit. A fretful or fearful heart drains the soul of precious strength, expending needless energy. But the contented heart builds and conserves strength.

We all know this intuitively, for in our moments of contentment we find great peace. Yet such occasions are all too fleeting, and it is the rare person who knows satisfaction as a familiar companion. We strive for more—more results, more comfort, more stuff—rather than resting in contentment.

Contentment isn't old-fashioned. It is quite biblical. "But godliness with contentment is great gain" (1 Timothy 6:6), the apostle Paul wrote his protégé, Timothy. In other words, we really won't enjoy a godly lifestyle apart from a healthy sense of spiritual well-being.

A mind at ease is perhaps the surest footing for a contented heart. "You will keep in perfect peace him whose mind is steadfast, because he trusts in you. Trust in the LORD forever, for the LORD, the LORD, is the Rock eternal" (Isaiah 26:3–4). God's peace of mind is for the people who trust confidently in the Lord's power and strength. Without faith, we have no peace that God will take care of us and our problems. The person whose mind is at rest, free from the distractions of inappropriate anxiety, has learned to put wholehearted faith in God's ability.

Contented people also gratefully acknowledge God as the generous Giver and learn to receive all gifts with humility and reverence. Eternal life is a gift from God. Every good thing we enjoy is a gift from the goodness of God (James 1:17). Whether we have little or much, our possessions are from the benevolent heart of God. There is no excuse for slackness or complacency, for work has its rewards—ultimately we must acknowledge the Lord as our Provider and Sustainer.

Pastor and author John Piper has written that "God is most glorified when we are most satisfied in him." Contentment feasts on making fellowship with Christ the sacred pursuit. The more you delight yourself in God, relishing your relationship as a child with your Father, the more you discover true contentment. When your satisfaction is derived from a personal relationship with the Father, the inevitable disappointments that life brings will do little damage, for you are held firm in the grip of the Father's steadfast, unconditional love, turning to him for lasting peace. He is all you need.

———— • ————

Father, I fall at your feet, resting in your strength. My heart is content in knowing you are there for me.

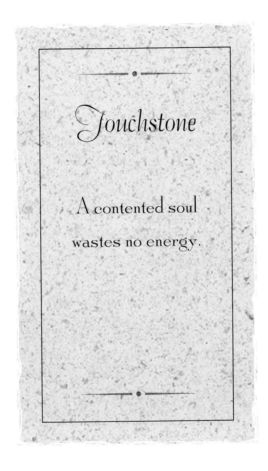

Touchstone

A contented soul

wastes no energy.

Good news gives health to the bones.

The Power of Encouragement

---

he teacher sensed the class had become disgruntled over some perplexing schoolwork. For a mental break, she asked the kids to put their books down, write something good about another student, and give it to that person after class.

Many years later the teacher attended a funeral for one of the students who was killed in the Vietnam War. The parents of the deceased student asked the teacher to come to their home following the funeral. When she arrived, they opened their son's wallet and handed her a carefully folded piece of paper. It was the note he had received from another student in her class. As friends gathered, several other students from the same class revealed that they, too, had kept their special slip of paper throughout the years.

What an amazing story about the power of encouragement. We all ache for a kind word, a tender touch. Remarks that foster a genuine sense of well-being can renew and strengthen even the weariest of souls.

The Greek word for *gospel* is literally translated "good news." The Scriptures are God's good news for humankind, celebrating the gift of eternal and abundant life in Jesus Christ. Each time we pick up the Bible and read it, we encounter the love of God. There are times of correction and sorrow, but even those instances are overshadowed by the great love God has for us (Hebrews 12:6).

The wonder of it all is that God thinks only good things about us. There is no condemnation for the Christian (Romans 8:1). Our lifestyle or behavior does not alter God's unconditional love for us. His loving-kindness, expressed to us in so many ways, is everlasting. God doesn't have anything negative to say about us because we are his possessions, purchased through the death of his Son. He says we are accepted, we are precious, we are more than conquerors through Christ. We can tuck away his promises in our hearts and carry them with us always. They will see us through any storm. They will sustain us in any heartache.

Knowing that God thinks only well of you should help you to encourage others. Do you know someone who is down, someone who is discouraged, someone who has been under a load and is bending beneath it? Find a way to bring kind, gentle, healing words to soothe the pain. Tell that person something good, something you admire about him or her. It could make a significant difference.

———— • ————

Dear Jesus, help me to be a drink of water to those who are thirsty for a loving, kind word. Bring to mind someone specific that I can reach out to. Strengthen the soul of this person through my encouraging words.

Touchstone

Let us encourage
one another.

My help comes from the LORD, the Maker of heaven and earth.

PSALM 121:2

Asking for God's Help

A plaque hanging in the study of pioneer missionary Hudson Taylor, reminded him daily of God's power as he shared the gospel in the heart of China. It was inscribed with these words: "Ebenezer" and "Jehovah-Jireh."

Ebenezer is the Hebrew word the prophet Samuel gave to the place where Israel gained a great victory over its enemies. The term literally means "stone of help," and Samuel celebrated the rout by proclaiming, "Thus far has the LORD helped us" (1 Samuel 7:12). *Jehovah-Jireh* is a compound name for God and means "God, my Provider." When Taylor looked at the pressing problems on the world's largest mission field, he saw them in the perspective of God's past help and promise of future provision.

The power of God is manifested in his sure and certain help to humankind. David often cried out to the Lord for his help (Psalm 18:6; 30:10; 54:4; 59:4; 124:8). Throughout the Scriptures, those in distress called on God for divine assistance. Although God's relief may not have come as quickly or predictably as they might have liked, he always heard their pleas for help.

When King Asa was staring at a bloodthirsty throng of Cushites bent on destroying Judah, he quickly realized his impotence. "Then Asa called to the LORD his God and said, 'LORD, there is no one like you to help the powerless against the mighty. Help us, O LORD our God, for we rely on you, and in your name we have come against this vast army'" (2 Chronicles 14:11). Asa surveyed the situation, recognized his inability, and came to God for help. Had he relied on the fighting spirit of his men—more than 300,000—he would have fallen. But his confession of inadequacy turned his attention to the Lord, and God gave him victory.

The fundamental criterion to receive God's help is an admission of our own helplessness. Only those who know they cannot be saved through their own righteous efforts realize their need for the Savior. Only they who grasp their own powerlessness to deal with a specific situation turn to the Lord for help. Catherine Marshall writes in her book *Adventures in Prayer*, "Why would God insist on helplessness as a prerequisite to answered prayer? One obvious reason is because our human helplessness is bedrock fact. God is a realist and insists that we be realists too. So long as we are deluding ourselves that human resources can supply our heart's desires, we are believing a lie."

If you focus only on your deficiency, and not on God's adequacy, you will seldom have the courage to rise above your circumstances. Seeking God's help is a confession of the Lord's majesty and power. The problem is severe, but God is sufficient. Others may fail you, but God will not, for he is the Sovereign Lord. He has helped you thus far, and he will not let you down now. Your help is in the Lord. Is there a better source?

———— ◆ ————

Mighty Lord, I can do nothing without your strength. Thank you for reminding me that all my power, all my knowledge is powerless without first being filtered through your strength.

Touchstone

We are weak, but
he is strong.

Yet I will rejoice in the LORD.

HABAKKUK 3:18

Trusting in God

We have all had bad days—maybe even bad weeks, months, or years. Things just don't go right. In fact, things grow worse, and nothing we do seems to alleviate the problems. The outlook is pessimistic, and our strength fades.

The writings of the prophet Habakkuk illustrate a time like this. Faced with the certain brutal conquest of his country Judah by his enemies the Babylonians, Habakkuk reels off the grim prospects of the hostile invasion: fig and olive tree would fail to yield fruit, the grape crop would fail, livestock would disappear—crippling the entire agrarian-based economy (3:17). The worst-case scenario seems about to happen, and Habakkuk is powerless to stop it.

At this crucial moment, while anxiety assaults his emotions (3:16), the prophet makes a decidedly spiritual turn. In spite of it all, he will "rejoice in the LORD" (3:18). Clearly something has changed Habakkuk's thinking. The gloom and doom of the previous verses are replaced by upbeat confidence in God. He knows the cruel days that await Judah, yet he refuses to succumb to a defeated spirit. The concluding verse to the prophet's discourse reveals the key to his spiritual shift: "The Sovereign LORD is my strength; he makes my feet like the feet of a deer, he enables me to go on the heights" (3:19).

When all else fails, Habakkuk affirms that a sovereign God who rules over all people and nations is the anchor for his trust. As bad as things are in Judah and as bad as they will become, God is trustworthy. When all else is out of control, the sovereign Lord is the One who is completely in control.

Such is our assurance. In good and bad, God is working everything out for his purposes (Romans 8:28). Nothing is outside God's power; therefore, no situation can thwart God's ultimate plans for our lives. And although current circumstances may belie the Lord's benevolence, his plans for us are good and pleasant (Jeremiah 29:11).

Knowing that God reigns over all that assails us and that he can and will work for good helps us make spiritual progress in times of testing. He encourages us to move on to a firmer faith, taking us to the heights of intimate fellowship with himself. Bad days, bad times are opportunities to see God work in our lives and trust him for the outcome.

If trials serve as occasions to more clearly see his hand at work in your life, then you are strengthened for the journey, ready for whatever may come. Your sovereign Lord knows the beginning from the end, and he will see you through.

———— • ————

Thank you, Father, that in your omniscience you knew about my circumstances before I ever did. You also know the outcome right now, and I'm trusting you through this time.

Touchstone

Not only can God see
through the storms,
he knows when they
are coming.

Where have you come from, and where are you going?

GENESIS 16:8

Obeying God's Word

It was the one thing she did not want to do: go back. Mistreated terribly by her mistress Sarah, Hagar had run away into the desert. The abuse she had taken must have been terrible because she fled into a hostile region where her chances for survival were slim. When we consider that she was also pregnant with her son, Ishmael, we can imagine her despair.

When she stopped by a brook, an angel of God spoke to Hagar. What he told her was not what she wanted to hear: "Go back to your mistress and submit to her" (Genesis 16:9). Can you imagine how she must have felt? "God, you want me to go back to a woman who has despised and wronged me? It was so bad, I'm out here in the burning desert to get away from her."

Even with some of the promises the angel made to Hagar regarding the lineage through her unborn son, the journey back to the camp of Sarah and Abraham must have been long and bitter. Had she correctly heard the angel? Would God do all the things he had pledged? How many more days could she endure Sarah's contempt?

We can learn several important lessons from the life of this Egyptian servant that will strengthen our faith and help us advance through our adversities.

Doing what God says, even when it doesn't make sense and involves some hardship on our part, is always the best choice. Obeying God when the puzzle pieces seem to fit nicely and the rewards are imminent isn't all that difficult. But following his guidance when it flies in the face of common sense is demanding.

Hagar had every good reason to keep moving on and only the angel's pronouncement to return.

When we do what God instructs us to do, we will eventually be blessed. Hagar's relationship with Sarah apparently didn't improve much; for, about fifteen years later, Hagar and her son were thrown out of Abraham's camp. Alone again in the desert and her son near death (Genesis 21:9–20), Hagar was once again ministered to by an angel. The angel miraculously provided for them and ultimately confirmed the Lord's compassionate promises.

The same principle of obedience and blessing is found in the lives of other Bible characters. Moses was not very keen on leading the Hebrews out of Egypt, even with the evidence of the burning bush. He preferred that someone else do the job—but obeyed despite his misgivings. Naaman, the Syrian leper who had come to Elisha for healing, ridiculed the prophet's simple prescription of bathing in the Jordan River. He soon reconsidered and was supernaturally healed. Each did what God asked, against their own inclinations, and discovered God's reward.

At the heart of it all is a submissive spirit. When we submit our will to God, we gain great power. At that moment, we proclaim that his purposes have a higher priority than ours and his agenda is the one that really counts. Look at the Lord's care for Hagar. She bowed in obedience, and he provided her every need.

Never hesitate to do what God asks in his Word, even when it goes against your grain. He knows what he has in mind, and you can never go wrong obeying the Lord. Do what he asks with a servant's heart, knowing that the Lord himself is your master. You will be amazed at the results.

Heavenly Father, forgive me whenever I try to walk according to the way of the world. Help me to discern your will; strengthen me for the journey.

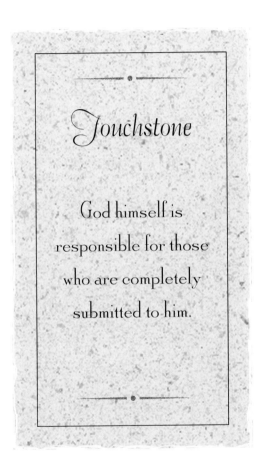

Touchstone

God himself is
responsible for those
who are completely
submitted to him.

It is good to praise the LORD and make music to your
name, O Most High, to proclaim your love in the
morning.

PSALM 92:1–2

Meditating on God's Word

---◦---

The extraordinary life of George Mueller is often remembered when addressing the topic of faith. His example of trust in God to provide the operating funds to support orphanages has long inspired me. Ministering in Bristol, England, Mueller ran as many as five orphanages that taught and trained two thousand children. There were no pledges of support, no well-known patrons, just daily provision of funds as Mueller brought the needs of the schools before God in prayer each morning.

Mueller's writings, compiled in *An Autobiography of George Mueller*, reveal a discovery he made that formed the foundation for his remarkable consistency in seeking God and his supply.

"My practice had been, at least for ten years previously, as an habitual thing, to give myself to prayer, after having dressed in the morning. Now I saw that the most important thing I had to do was to give myself to the reading of the Word of God and to meditation on it, that thus my heart might be comforted, encouraged, warned, reproved, instructed; and that thus, whilst meditating, my heart might be brought into experiential communion with the Lord. I began therefore, to meditate on the New Testament, from the beginning, early in the morning."

Meditation on Scripture became the lifelong practice and source of strength for Mueller, and I still marvel at the results a century later. But Mueller is no exception. The power of meditating on the Word of God is just as potent for the believer today as it was for him. The Bible is full of life, truth, wisdom, and power, available to all who are willing to drink from its fountain.

As Joshua prepared to fill Moses' shoes and take the Hebrews to their original destination, Canaan, the Lord clearly revealed to

Joshua the secret to his success: "This book of the law shall not depart out of your mouth, but you shall meditate on it day and night, that you may be careful to do according to all that is written in it; for then you shall make your way prosperous, and then you shall have good success" (Joshua 1:8 RSV).

Joshua's strength for battle, Mueller's fuel for faith, our manna for daily encounters is meditation on the Word of God. Reading the Bible is essential for understanding God's mind. Studying Scripture is crucial for a balanced, mature faith; meditating on the promises of God is the catalyst for a dynamic personal faith. When we mull over what God has said, asking him what he is saying to us, we write the Word on our hearts.

Meditation is lingering on the verse, hearing what God is saying to our unique, individual circumstances and how we may apply the truth to our endeavors, problems, and challenges. Meditation soaks our lives in the supernatural power of the Scripture.

Mueller's discovery of the priority of meditating on the Word of God changed his life: "By the blessing of God I ascribe to this mode the help and strength which I have had from God to pass in peace through deeper trials in various ways than I had ever had before; and after having now above forty years tried this way, I can most fully, in the fear of God, commend it."

God's Word is food for the inner self, the godly nourishment that sustains and satisfies. Meditate consistently on it, and you will feed your faith in amazing ways.

———— • ————

Lord Jesus, help me to start each day in your strength. As I wake each morning, prompt my spirit to open your Word.

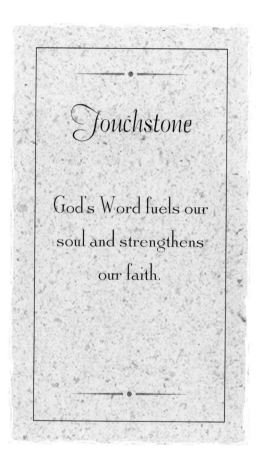

Touchstone

God's Word fuels our
soul and strengthens
our faith.

I press on to take hold of that for which Christ Jesus took hold of me.

PHILIPPIANS 3:12

A Sense of Mission

Thousands of sorties were flown during the Persian Gulf War. In many cases, pilots flew several raids each day, taxing physical and mental capabilities. What kept the pilots alert and focused in the grueling demands of war was the compelling sense of mission. Each sortie had a defined target and objective.

A clear mission and purpose for the believer is a powerful spiritual element for continued growth and fruitfulness. The Christian who walks aimlessly about each day, wondering what to do, will seldom reach satisfying spiritual heights.

Jesus had a crystalline sense of mission. Early in his ministry, as he healed the sick and delivered the demon-possessed, the crowds begged him to stay. Jesus knew he must move on. "I must preach the good news of the kingdom of God to the other towns also, because that is why I was sent" (Luke 4:43). As his crucifixion neared, Jesus repeated his divine objective: "We are going up to Jerusalem, and the Son of Man will be betrayed to the chief priests and the teachers of the law. They will condemn him to death and will turn him over to the Gentiles to be mocked and flogged and crucified. On the third day he will be raised to life!" (Matthew 20:18–19).

The apostle Paul was thoroughly harassed, threatened, and beaten as he took the gospel to the Gentiles. His sense of mission left no room for detours. "However, I consider my life worth nothing to me, if only I may finish the race and complete the task the Lord Jesus has given me—the task of testifying to the gospel of God's grace" (Acts 20:24).

All disciples of Christ, each uniquely equipped and gifted, have a similar overarching mission—to glorify Christ in all they do. We are here for a specific purpose, to honor God in our words, deeds, thoughts, and lifestyles. "And whatever you do, whether in word or deed, do it all in the name of the Lord Jesus" (Colossians 3:17). We are called to do our work, family activities, hobbies—everything—with the express purpose of glorifying Jesus Christ.

When our mission is lucid—to glorify God—we cultivate the kind of stamina and perseverance needed for a God-honoring life. There are dangers and difficulties ahead, but the Christian with a focused mission can keep pressing onward and Godward.

The challenge is to personalize that mission with clear goals. You must ask yourself: How can I honor God in my finances, my job, my relationships? The answers should be practical, prayerful steps you can pursue daily. Writing down these specific, measurable, attainable goals is one spiritual exercise that will pay great dividends.

———— ❖ ————

Lord Jesus, help me this week to set clearly definable goals in each area of my life that will glorify you and further your kingdom.

Touchstone

If you aim at nothing,

you seldom miss.

O Lord, hear my prayer, listen to my cry for mercy;
in your faithfulness and righteousness come to my
relief.

PSALM 143:1

The Power of Prayer

---

*J*onah found himself in the stomach of a whale and prayed. King Jehoshaphat was surrounded by hostile armies and prayed. Hannah was childless and prayed. Paul and Silas were in a Roman prison and prayed. The disciples asked Jesus to teach them about one important thing—how to pray.

The power of prayer is the backbone for a vigorous, profitable Christian life. I don't know of any spiritual exercise more experientially powerful than personal, prevailing prayer. Anyone can pray. At anytime. About anything.

Prayer works, I believe, for two very important reasons. Prayer admits our need for God to act on our behalf, and prayer focuses on God as the ultimate problem solver.

As long as we can solve problems through the usual means, our prayer life is usually mundane. Phrases like "God bless Grandma and Grandpa today" become the staple of our conversations with the Lord. There is a triteness and smallness to our prayer life. Of course, the Lord wants us to pray about everything, common and uncommon; he wants us to understand that we are quite dependent on him.

When we voice our concerns, desires, and distresses to the Lord in prayer, we take a potent step to admitting our great need for God. We can't make our teenager stop doing drugs. We can't force our boss to respect us. However, when we pray about such pressing things, we admit our own inadequacy and our inability to control the circumstances. Jonah couldn't escape from his denizen of the deep. Jehoshaphat couldn't defeat superior forces. Hannah couldn't create a child. Paul and Silas couldn't shatter leg irons. But they could pray. God could answer—and he did.

Calling out to God, recognizing our reliance on him, is only part of the equation however. Understanding our need for the Lord sets prayer in motion, but turning to Christ as the problem solver shifts the burden from our shoulders to his. Prayer is not only about our frailty but also about God's staggering might, care, and wisdom.

Prayer doesn't work because of the intensity or frequency of our petitions. Prayer works because of who we pray to. All-sufficient God himself is the person who hears and responds to our pleas, moans, and appeals. God alone has the divine power to arrange circumstances and events, to work in the hearts of men and women to accomplish his will. God delivered Jonah, destroyed Jehoshaphat's foes, opened Hannah's womb, and shattered Paul and Silas's chains.

God did it, and he is the same God who will come to your aid today when you call on his name and seek his will. Take your matters to him and put the problem squarely on his magnificent shoulders. Wait on his reply and his direction. He will move heaven and earth to work on your behalf and honor his name.

Father, I can do nothing without you. My strength lies with you in all my circumstances. I lay each one at your feet right now and trust you with the details and outcome.

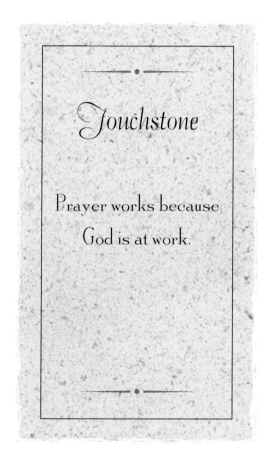

Touchstone

Prayer works because
God is at work.

Therefore, there is now no condemnation for those who are in Christ Jesus.

ROMANS 8:1

Strength Through Failure

⬤

$\mathcal{T}$hings looked bleak for a U.S. commander in the Second World War: his troops, the first under his command, hit the shores of North Africa hoping to conquer the German troops. But shortly after a quick beachhead, they were met with a stinging defeat at the hand of Rommel's army—thousands of the commander's infantrymen were killed and hundreds of his tanks lost. The mission was a complete failure.

Only a few years later, the Allied forces appointed this very man the Supreme Commander of their armies in the European theater. And, less than ten years after his great failure in North Africa, he was elected President of the United States.

Dwight D. Eisenhower had overcome the bitter taste of early defeat on his road to military and political accolades.

We, too, can see our failures work together for good (Romans 8:28) through the infinite wisdom and kindness of God. The episodes that we would consider disappointing, even crushing, can have redemptive qualities in God's rich scheme of grace.

Think about the lives of biblical figures. Abraham lied about his wife's identity to save himself. Moses murdered a man. David was an adulterer and killer. The disciples fled after Christ's crucifixion. The failures of humankind mark the pages of Scripture, yet they aren't the sinkholes that we imagine. God specializes in picking us up out of the pit and restoring our confidence.

Sometimes failure is our responsibility. We have sinned. We caused the problem. The blame falls squarely on us. This can be the deadliest form of failure since self-judgment can be severe.

Looking at our debacle, we turn our anger toward ourselves, condemning our actions far more critically than God does. God doesn't hold any grudges against us; rather, he offers the gift of forgiveness—we can escape the trap of self-condemnation simply by accepting his gift.

On other occasions, the failure is the result of circumstances beyond our control. Debilitating consequences can knock us down emotionally and precipitate responses such as depression and anger. In these instances, we must grasp the comforting truth that God is in control, despite the adversity. We are not at the mercy of the economy or the actions of others; rather, we are to put our trust in the God who controls all things.

Failure is never final with God because with him all things are possible. If we fall, he will pick us up. If we falter, he will come to our rescue. Our greatest triumphs can be achieved if we learn to turn to the Lord in the midst of failure. Instead of spiraling downward to misery, we can partake of God's peace and comfort. Instead of sinking into self-pity, we can learn that our self-worth is anchored in our identity as God's children.

Don't let failure keep you down. God stands ready to pick you up, and he uses your failures to mature your faith and draw you into a more intimate fellowship with him. He never condemns you.

———— ◆ ————

Lord Jesus, sometimes I really do feel like a failure. It doesn't take much, at times, for me to get down on myself. Help me to memorize your promises from Scripture to keep me focused on your truth and how much you value me.

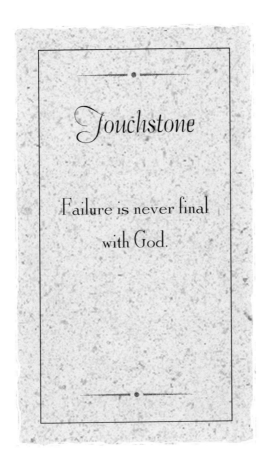

Touchstone

Failure is never final
with God.

God is our refuge and strength.

PSALM 46:1

Our Hiding Place

     ⬤

There are certain events, no matter how well prepared we are spiritually, that simply slam us hard to the ground and take our breath away. We may have been fighting the good fight of faith with growing confidence or making great headway on the road to spiritual maturity, then unexpected news hits with punishing, unnerving fury. We feel unable to withstand the blow and our knees buckle.

There is only one thing to do in these jolting moments—take refuge in the Lord Jesus Christ. The psalmist repeatedly uses the language of refuge: God is our hiding place, fortress, stronghold, shield, and rock. He is the one to whom we run when evil threatens to undo us. He is the place of security and protection when we feel exceedingly vulnerable. In these perilous times, we should never try to rely on our own strength and stamina. God, however, is ever ready to be our place of sanctuary.

We must come to him quickly. The swell of emotions, particularly fear, grows exceedingly fast; the longer we nurture the feelings, the more powerful they become. Hesitation is dangerous. We need to turn to God immediately, admit our bewilderment and shock, and ask him to cover us in this precarious time.

I know of a pastor who lost his son in a freak boating accident while the family was on a church retreat. The pastor was in a small cottage when a church friend came to the door and told him his son had been killed. Instantly, the pastor dropped to his knees and cried out to God to help him make it through the devastation of loss. The pastor spent years grieving over the death of his son, often spending nights pacing his long driveway in anguished conversations with God. The Lord saw him through the pain, and I am convinced that his spontaneous plea for God's help was honored.

Coming quickly to God is the act of a saint who knows that only the Lord can help him. Friends and family can offer words of encouragement, but at times God alone must suffice. As David cried out, "My soul finds rest in God alone; my salvation comes from him. He alone is my rock and my salvation; he is my fortress, I will never be shaken.... Find rest, O my soul, in God alone; my hope comes from him" (Psalm 62:1–2, 5).

Make God your "ever-present help in trouble" (Psalm 46:1) because he is the mighty fortress against the fury of evil. When you take refuge in him, he comforts and cares for you, strengthening you for the battle. "Therefore we will not fear, though the earth give way and the mountains fall into the heart of the sea, though its waters roar and foam and the mountains quake with their surging" (Psalm 46:2).

———— ◦ ————

Thank you, Father, that no matter what rages against me, you will never abandon or forsake me. You will always be there.

Touchstone

Only God is mightier
than the storms
of life.

God has made me fruitful in the land of my suffering.

GENESIS 41:52

Wounds that Heal

Matt Luke is a professional baseball player. He is also a man who has learned a powerful lesson through years of personal adversity.

As a young boy, Luke endured the taunts and teasings of playmates due to a facial disfigurement. He learned to ignore the jeers and went on to become a star athlete, eventually playing on a major league team. Even though several operations corrected much of the distortions, facial scars still were faintly visible. Luke could have undergone further cosmetic surgery to eliminate all traces of his affliction, but he chose not to. When asked about his decision, Luke responded with this pointed remark: "I have become the person I am today because of my scars." Luke refused to let the crude remarks be obstacles in his personal development, instead using them as incentive to greater achievement.

We all have scars to mark the wounds we have suffered as a result of our own harmful behavior or from the painful actions or words of others. Many times we try to forget about them, ignore them, or suppress them. These strategies are seldom effective and evade a central issue of the Christian life: suffering. God can use our pain to strengthen us and develop our character.

Joseph, who spent thirteen long years in Egyptian servitude and imprisonment before becoming its second most powerful leader, named his second son Ephraim, which means "twice fruitful." The name reminded Joseph that God had woven his sufferings into a beautifully designed plan. Joseph became the godly man he was created to be because of his sufferings, not in spite of them.

Think about the apostle Paul. He had plenty of scars: the physical kind, from brutal lashings and angry stonings; and the kind you don't see, from rejection by his own people and loneliness from years of unjust imprisonment. But Paul became the great apostle of the gospels through his sufferings, with many of his epistles inked in the dim light of a jail.

Our scars can help us become the people of God we were created to become and can even help us accomplish feats unattainable apart from our ordeals. Joseph chose to trust in God's sovereign plan for his life. Speaking to his brothers who had betrayed and sold him, he emphatically stated: "You intended to harm me, but God intended it for good" (Genesis 50:20). Paul refused to look back bitterly on his problems; instead he exclaimed that he would "press on toward the goal to win the prize for which God has called me heavenward in Christ Jesus" (Philippians 3:14).

God will use your scars as part of his healing process to conform you to the image of Christ, to produce in you that indomitable spirit of faith and courage in God's sovereign plan. Remember, too, that one day when you meet Christ face-to-face, you will see the scars that made him your Savior.

———— • ————

Father, show me how to overcome the afflictions of my scars. I'm trusting you now for the victory and the joy that will result from them.

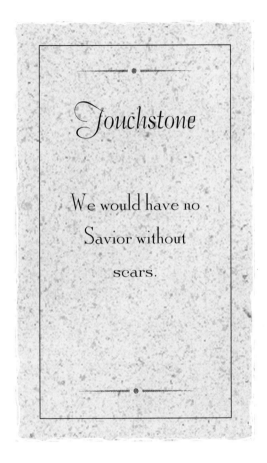

Touchstone

We would have no
Savior without

scars.

Who despises the day of small things?

ZECHARIAH 4:10

Step by Step

Orporate recruiters who visit college campuses today to interview prospective employees universally complain that students want everything immediately. Students want to start with an impressive title, lots of perks, and a hefty salary. They want to climb the ladder in one giant leap.

That doesn't work in God's scheme—or in the world's either, for that matter. We gain strength for greater future challenges by demonstrating faithfulness in the routine rounds of everyday living.

My Bible teaching ministry began in a small town in the mountains of North Carolina. The Bible institute where I taught and the church that I pastored were quite unpretentious. Like any eager young pastor, I sometimes thought about moving on to bigger churches.

I still clearly remember God's plain message to me that laid the foundation for my future ministry. Listening to a pastor at the Bible institute talk rather smugly about his ministry in a large church, I realized that God hated pride and was pleased by a humble, obedient spirit. That day, I promised God that I would remain in that rural community for the rest of my life if that was his will.

God did eventually lead me to other places, but I learned a crucial scriptural lesson applicable to everyone who wants to serve and honor God: If we want to succeed in our walk with Christ and be productive in all our work, we must be faithful in the small things.

If our goal is to run a marathon, we begin by running a few miles. If our aim is to save for retirement, we achieve it by setting aside a little money from each paycheck. Strength for the journey is gained step by step, deed by deed, day by day.

God is looking for consistency in the mundane, small things of life because he wants us to work for his honor, not ours. We are easily captivated by our own importance, and that is a definite hindrance to doing things God's way. There weren't very many people who listened to me preach each Sunday in that tiny mountain town years ago, but I was just as responsible then to study, pray, and prepare as I am now. If I preached to please men, then I would not be pleasing God.

The Lord wants us to be faithful in the small things as much as in the big things because he knows we need to be seasoned in our character and spirit. People who want to skyrocket to the top without paying their dues probably will tumble because they haven't developed the necessary level of maturity. The lessons learned in applying God's truth to our daily struggles strengthen us for larger undertakings. It takes time for saints to grow.

Never underestimate the power of small steps of obedience. They pave the way to God's wonderful plan for the future.

———— ◆ ————

Lord, help me to have the right attitude as you grow me up in my walk with you. Teach me to be patient and honorable in the small things so that you may achieve great things through me.

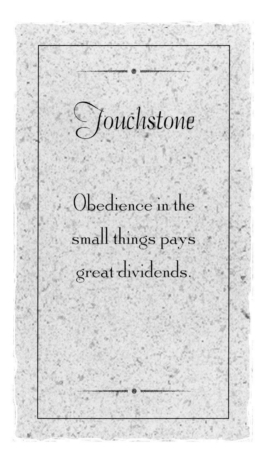

Touchstone

Obedience in the
small things pays
great dividends.

If anyone serves, he should do it with the strength God provides.

1 PETER 4:11

Power to Serve

⊙

---

*J*esus, the sovereign Lord, was also the perfect servant. Christ, the King who could have demanded and secured obedience, instead chose to serve.

We struggle in this facet of the spiritual life more than almost any other aspect. So often "the spirit is willing, but the flesh is weak." We do try to serve: We take up good, noble causes at church and work; we put our shoulder to the task—and then find ourselves stumbling, flagging, and faltering. Our level of service to the community of believers and others frequently diminishes, not increases, with the passing of time. We burn out. We try to lift others around us and find ourselves weighted down in the process.

Peter, who at first served by his own strength, told us later that we must serve "with the strength God provides." The power for service, like any other demand in our faith walk, comes from Jesus Christ. Maybe Peter was thinking of his earlier, botched attempts at serving the Lord when he penned these words and wanted to keep others from repeating his mistakes.

Serving in God's strength is possible when we learn to work in the area of our giftedness. God has given each believer spiritual gifts (Romans 12:6; 1 Corinthians 12:4). The Holy Spirit confers these gifts and empowers us to use them effectively. If we don't know the gifts that God has equipped us to serve with, then we will constantly wrestle with genuine servanthood.

Those who are gifted by the Holy Spirit with the talent for teaching enjoy helping others learn. Individuals who possess the gift of administration love to organize, plan, and achieve. We are all called to a lifestyle of service, but the most effective servants are those who operate in their area of giftedness in the church. The more they serve, the more fulfilled they are.

We serve in God's strength when we seek to honor Christ above all else. Peter said to serve in God's strength so that "in all things God may be praised through Jesus Christ" (1 Peter 4:11). If service is motivated only to please ourselves, we haven't gripped the biblical model of servanthood at all. All service is for the glory of Christ, to bring *him* applause and attention, not ourselves. If we use our gifts to gain personal recognition, we are no servants of Christ. People will disappoint us; God never fails to acknowledge our service to him.

God's power to serve is best employed when we think as he does. Our culture demeans the servant, while God promises to exalt and bless the believer who serves humbly and loyally. Christ is always turning the world's thinking upside down: Jesus served as he suffered, and he set the role for every true believer. Finding his strength in the common rounds of servanthood requires we adopt his mind. His ways are different than ours, and we are best equipped to discover those ways as servants.

Discover your spiritual gifts, perhaps by asking other believers what they feel you do best; and then develop and use your gifts. You will gain power for service when you realize that every act of service to others is for Christ's sake. Live and serve to the praise of his glory. If you deeply desire to honor the Lord, you will find the strength to serve in the most troubling and humbling of times.

———— ❖ ————

Dear Jesus, help me to discover my spiritual gifts so that I may more effectively serve you. Thank you for supernaturally equipping me to do your work.

Touchstone

The Servant, himself,

gives us a

servant's heart.

I worked harder than all of them—yet not I, but the grace of God that was with me.

1 CORINTHIANS 15:10

The Divine Tension

———— ◆ ————

A divine tension exists between the strength God supplies for our tasks and the strength we supply. What is God's part, and what is our part?

The apostle Paul worked around the clock wherever he ministered. By day, and often by night, the eminent preacher stitched together rough, heavy pieces of fabric to make tents. When he wasn't plying his trade, he was teaching the Scriptures to the church, defending the gospel to the critics, and evangelizing the lost.

Paul looked at his efforts in this light: "To this end I labor, struggling with all his energy, which so powerfully works in me" (Colossians 1:29).

At first glance, Paul's statement almost seems a contradiction. But it expresses the spiritual equilibrium that is required for sound Christian living.

Paul "labored" as he worked and preached. The Greek word picture is one of toil and sweat, with a deep sense of weariness. This is a portrait of a man who is bone tired at the end of the day. Not only did he labor, he "struggled." In other words, few things came easy. The work of taking Christ to the nations was hard and painful, exacting a mental and physical toll on the apostle.

So why did he not break? How did he continue crossing continents and seas without faltering? And just as critical a question, how can we go about our demanding lives without collapsing under the load?

Paul did all he could, but he never viewed his ventures as an individual undertaking. It was Paul at work in cities and fields, but not Paul alone. Rather, he approached his tasks by drawing on "God's energy" that "powerfully worked" on his behalf. Undergirding all of his enterprises was the great power of God, silently but supernaturally enabling all he did.

Our part, like Paul's, is to put forth all the effort we can muster. God ordained work at creation; it has been made painful by sin, but work is still his idea. We are to pray, think, investigate, plan, prepare, and do whatever else we have the ability to do as we go about our business. God will not usurp our responsibility.

None of this is done, however, without God's full participation. We do not act independently of Christ's indwelling power. In all we do, in dependence on him, God is actively working to accomplish his purposes and do his will. We can count on his wisdom, his love, his grace, and his mercy.

The final outcome rests in his hands. He must be the one to crown our efforts with success. When we "commit to the LORD whatever [we] do" (our part), "[our] plans will succeed" (God's part) (Proverbs 16:3).

Do all you can, and trust God to do all he can.

———— ● ————

Lord, give me your supernatural energy to accomplish your plan for my life and through my life. I give you all that I am and all that I'll be for your service.

Touchstone

God cannot do

our part, and

we cannot

do his.

Be still, and know that I am God.

PSALM 46:10

Strength in Letting Go

The daughter of one of America's greatest authors, Nathaniel Hawthorne, lay in a bed on the verge of death as malaria coursed wildly through her body. Hawthorne had become despondent. "I cannot endure the alternations of hope and fear; therefore, I have settled with myself not to hope at all."

Hawthorne's wife still hoped that God would intervene, and she prayed for God's healing. Bending over the frail body of her daughter, Mrs. Hawthorne gave the matter to God: "Why should I doubt the goodness of God. Let him take Una, if he sees best. More than that: I can give her to him! I do give her to you, Lord. I won't fight you anymore." Only a few minutes later, Una's fever abated, and she made a complete recovery.

Hawthorne had submitted to the most vile of emotions—hopelessness—while his wife had made a great discovery—the power of relinquishment. When encountering circumstances where the consequences can be monumental, we have the same options: we can bow to despair or quietly but emphatically submit our lives to God.

But should we not wrestle in prayer and put our whole-hearted trust in God? Yes. Should we not intensely seek the mind and will of God? Definitely. But that done, there is a time when we must relinquish the outcome of our circumstances to God. We have done all we can; the rest is in the hands of the Lord.

This is not resignation or abandonment to fate. Releasing our circumstances to the Lord is a mature step of faith, indicating our trust in the wisdom, goodness, and power of God. Arriving at that point is seldom easy, for there is always the feeling that we can do at least one more thing to solve our dilemma.

Still, God often waits for the person who, while continuing to seek and obey him at every turn, relinquishes the eventual results to him. Like Mrs. Hawthorne, we "give" our situation to the Lord. We commit the matter into his capable hands. We cease from striving after our own solutions and are willing to accept his.

Perhaps he will give us what we ask, deliver us from what ails us, change the hearts of those opposed to us. But perhaps not. God wants our trust, but he does not need our help. Since our problems are matters of great concern to him, he will always deal rightly with what we entrust to his care.

Give whatever bothers you, whatever threatens you, whatever assaults you to God. He knows what to do.

———— • ————

Father, I really do struggle with a pessimistic outlook at times. When I see no logical way out of a situation, I'm slow to trust you. Forgive my attitude, and help me to realize you have the power to fix anything.

Touchstone

God can turn

your can'ts

into cans.

I have made you and I will carry you; I will sustain you and I will rescue you.

ISAIAH 46:4

After a Little While

Sir Winston Churchill spoke to the residents of Leeds, England, thirty-three months into the grueling Second World War. Sensing their weariness, the masterful orator turned their gaze to the future: "We shall go forward together. The road upward is stony. There are upon our journey dark and dangerous valleys through which we have to make and fight our way. But it is sure and certain that if we persevere—and we persevere—we shall come through these dark and dangerous valleys into a sunlight broader and more genial and more lasting than mankind has ever known."

The apostle Peter shares the biblical perspective while writing to a group of persecuted and probably discouraged Jews. "And the God of all grace, who called you to his eternal glory in Christ, after you have suffered a little while, will himself restore you and make you strong" (1 Peter 5:10).

The Bible is a riveting book of realism. It never denies or ignores our troubles. Yet it always offers the transcendent truth of God's presence and power during our frequent bouts with pain. We have many "dangerous valleys" and "stony paths" to traverse, but with God's enabling, we can endure.

Crucial to our steadfastness is knowing that the "God of all grace" is working on our behalf. Grace means we get better than we deserve. Grace is God working for our good when we experience evil, keeping us strong when we are weak, promoting peace when we are troubled. Grace is God's love overwhelming the obstacles and overcoming the odds. Grace is the Lord's refreshing rivers of plenty flowing into our barren places. We haven't earned it or sought it, but it is ours to receive.

Our God of grace has called us to "eternal glory." Whatever our current lot, we can be sure that a magnificent end is certain. The perpetual bliss of eternity will be ours one day. We can console ourselves with the assurance that God's ultimate plan for our lives is so exceedingly good that words can't justly describe it. The pieces of the puzzle may perplex us for now, but they will all fit together perfectly in the end. Eternity with Christ is surely a "sunlight more broad and genial" than we have ever known.

The suffering we now bear is not forever. God knows how much we can stand and will come to our aid in "a little while." At the right moment, maybe after months, maybe after years, God promises to restore and strengthen us. He brings relief as only he can to keep us from falling headlong into utter despair. God will sustain us when we think we are at our breaking point. He will revive us when our body and spirit are exhausted and spent.

When you are weary, put your hope in the Lord. Accept his grace and his strength to see you through these hard days.

I praise you, Lord, because you know me better than I know myself. You know what I can handle and you've promised to take care of me and never give me a load heavier than I can handle.

Touchstone

We need never

give up, because

God never gives

up on us.

[He] is able to do immeasurably more than all we ask or imagine, according to his power that is at work within us.

EPHESIANS 3:20

Jars of Clay

---

eople, says the Lord, are like clay. This analogy fascinates me, especially when I consider how common an element clay was in biblical times.

The prophet Isaiah made this comparison: "Yet, O LORD, you are our Father. We are the clay, you are the potter; we are all the work of your hand" (Isaiah 64:8). Jeremiah the prophet said that God the potter has the right to do with us as he pleases—shaping, remaking us into the vessel of his choosing (Jeremiah 18:1–10).

Paul picks up the analogy in his letter to the Romans (Romans 9:21), but his most striking use is in his second letter to the Corinthian church. "But we have this treasure," Paul writes, "in jars of clay to show that this all-surpassing power is from God and not from us" (2 Corinthians 4:7). For the most part, our lives are quite ordinary. We have our exceptional moments, but we spend the majority of our lives in predictable, customary pursuits and activities. But there is nothing mundane about what God is doing within us and through us. Our ordinary lives are the proving ground for God's extraordinary works of power.

God wants people to look to him, not to us. God works through our imperfect lives in such a compassionate way that people will be attracted to his kind and mighty presence. A woman who endured an abusive childhood with cruel and demanding parents is a broken jar through which God's love can be poured. A child with a physical or emotional handicap is marred clay through which the adequacy of Christ can be majestically displayed. A man with chronic illness can provide a workshop for the peace and joy of Jesus.

The divine hand of God is at work in our flawed and damaged lives—we are imperfect, but we have Perfection dwelling in our hearts. There, in our inner sanctuary, inside this jar of clay, God is renewing us day by day (2 Corinthians 4:16). He is strengthening us with power so that we can experience Jesus (Ephesians 1:17).

There is priceless treasure within us, the very presence and person of Jesus Christ. His life was broken and poured out for our sake. As we are broken for the sake of his kingdom, God himself is poured out through us—jars of clay—to others in need.

Take some time to discover how God is using your brokenness to bring wholeness. Refresh yourself by welcoming God's Spirit within you.

———— ❖ ————

Heavenly Father, I want to yield myself to your artistry. Mold me and shape me so that I may serve you and honor you in my life.

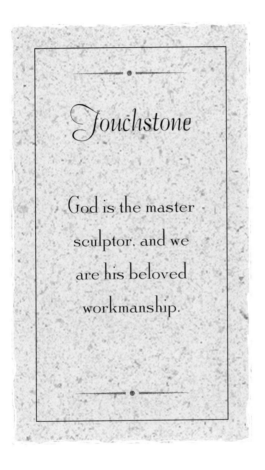

Touchstone

God is the master
sculptor, and we
are his beloved
workmanship.

And those who walk in pride he is able to humble.

DANIEL 4:37

Strength Through Humility

---

*I*nordinate self-sufficiency is a deadly enemy of God's power. Although our journey to physical and social self-reliance begins when we are children and gathers momentum as we reach adulthood, the spiritual journey is inverted—from independence to dependence.

King Uzziah's reign over Judah began auspiciously. He conquered enemies, restored important buildings, improved the agrarian economy, and built a superior fighting force. So far so good. But something happened along the way to notoriety. Uzziah developed a conceited spirit. Earlier, he had constantly sought the Lord, but as his reputation grew, so did his pride. "His fame spread far and wide, for he was greatly helped until he became powerful" (2 Chronicles 26:15).

Excessive pride turns our attention away from God and to ourselves. It disorients our spiritual bearings by putting our focus on our own magnetic efforts, putting us on the slippery slope of egotism, where "I" reigns instead of God.

C. S. Lewis wrote in *Mere Christianity*, "According to Christian teachers, the essential vice, the utmost evil, is Pride. Unchastity, anger, greed, drunkenness, and all that, are mere flea bites in comparison . . . pride leads to every other vice." Pride is such a dangerous foe because it takes the credit away from God and deposits it to our account. Our inflated notion of *self* distorts our view of God and seeks to honor our own accomplishments instead of glorifying Christ.

King Uzziah's early achievements were initially centered around a healthy, reverent relationship with God. He looked to the Lord for results, and God blessed his effort: "He sought God during the days of Zechariah, who instructed him in the fear of God. As long as he sought the LORD, God gave him success" (2 Chronicles 26:5).

Slowly and subtly, however, which is usually how pride works, Uzziah forgot the Lord. He looked at his empire and glowed over his feats. At some point, God's help ceased and Uzziah's behavior turned bizarre (2 Chronicles 26:16–23).

God grants us success. He delights in our accomplishments. But these can never come at the expense of losing intimacy with him due to a vainglorious spirit. The remedy for a heart hardened with pride is an honest, sincere appreciation of God's greatness. We may be bright and clever, but can we match the wisdom of God? We can do much, but how much more can God do? We may be capable of some very noble things, but with God all things are possible. This is all a proper "fear of God"—not a frightful, apprehensive view, but a reverent, holy understanding that God rules. The fear of the Lord breeds a humble spirit that acknowledges God as the Source of all.

Honor God and he will honor you.

Please forgive me, Lord, for the times pride has taken control of my life. Search me, know, and reveal to me any area that I need to surrender to you.

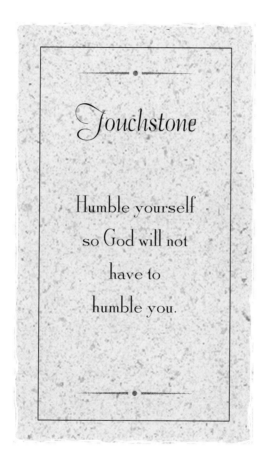

Touchstone

Humble yourself
so God will not
have to
humble you.

The Lord stood at my side and gave me strength.

2 TIMOTHY 4:17

The Power of His Promises

⸻ ❖ ⸻

*S*tanding alone takes strength. Standing against peers, against problems, against almost anything takes incredible strength. That's why the last chapter of 2 Timothy, Paul's last letter, is so intriguing. Paul was in prison again, and he knew that the end was near (4:6). He had already faced a preliminary trial and was awaiting a final hearing.

Most of his friends had either deserted him or were scattered abroad. Apparently, only Luke, the doctor and familiar companion, was with him in his last days. The sense of abandonment was keen, but it did not leave Paul hopeless. He writes of his first defense before his captors that "the Lord stood at my side and gave me strength" (4:17).

I've often wondered when I've read that passage how the Lord imparted his strength to Paul. What did the apostle mean about the Lord being at his side, and is there any application for us now?

One day, while reading the book of Acts, I came across a verse that provides some very helpful insight into what Paul may have experienced. Arrested in Jerusalem, the apostle was lodged in Roman barracks after his speech to his Jewish accusers had incited a near riot. Something supernatural then happened: "The following night the Lord stood near Paul and said, 'Take courage! As you have testified about me in Jerusalem, so you must also testify in Rome'" (Acts 23:11).

God stood near Paul, spoke to him, and the apostle was encouraged. He must have thought about the Lord's brief but powerful message when, the next day, a plot by the Jews to kill him was uncovered. That night he was whisked away to Caesarea, where he spent two years in confinement before arriving in Rome.

I don't know how God spoke to Paul. Perhaps the messenger was an angel, or maybe Paul heard directly from the Father. But here is the wonderful news for us today: The Lord can come near to us and stand at our side to strengthen us through the promises of Scripture.

God has spoken to us through his Word, and his powerful promises break through the night and pierce our loneliness with his comfort and cheer. We don't need an angel. We have the written revelation of God to tell us all we need to know, and the Lord can bring his encouraging words to our mind at exactly the right moment so that we don't faint.

I really do think this is how Paul was strengthened in moments of supreme difficulty. When there was no one else to help him, the Scripture was there to revive and refresh him. The promises of the Bible do the same for the weary, troubled saint today.

If you feel alone and need an encouraging word, ask the Lord to lead you to a verse of Scripture. Somehow, he will bring it to your attention, and you will be supernaturally strengthened.

———— ◆ ————

Thank you, Father, for the encouragement and comfort your Word has brought to me so many times. There is nothing this world has to offer that has helped me more. It is because you know us so well that you've provided for us so abundantly.

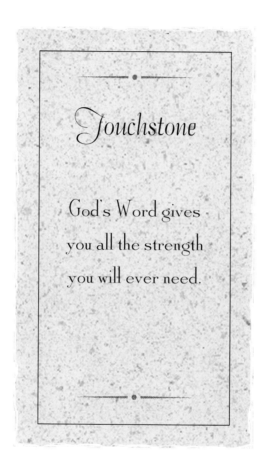

Touchstone

God's Word gives
you all the strength
you will ever need.

Let us throw off everything that hinders and the sin
that so easily entangles, and let us run with perseverance the race marked out for us.

HEBREWS 12:1

Easing the Load

------- ❋ -------

*L*ethargy is a deadly enemy of stamina and strength. Spiritual sluggishness is likewise the debilitating foe of godliness, sapping the soul with mediocrity and inertia. You can't grow strong for the seasons of life if you're a spiritual couch potato.

The problem is that many well-intentioned Christians who are caught in the doldrums don't know exactly how they got there or how to extricate themselves. They want to press on to know God, but progress is minimal. They're really not slackers, but they can't sustain much spiritual momentum.

God stands ready to supply his power in these instances once we realize we have the vital role of preparing our hearts to receive his strength. Notice the author's use of "let us" in Hebrews 12:1. With a demanding course set before us, we have a crucial responsibility for spiritual conditioning. "Let us throw off everything that hinders and the sin that so easily entangles."

Every photograph in this book was taken with cameras that I carried in a nifty backpack. I didn't mind the extra weight when needed, but if I toted that weight around while I preached or worked, I would get pretty tired.

I wonder how many Christians are weighted down with excess, extraneous baggage. I'm talking about emotional loads like anger, bitterness, or unforgiveness. They bog us down in our walk with Christ. They distract our pursuit of God. Through the convicting ministry of the Holy Spirit, God often pinpoints areas of sin in our lives. In response, we are to "throw off" these encumbrances through confession and repentance. We won't be able to run with vigor until we do.

After spending time with the Lord and asking him to release us from ungodly or unprofitable thoughts and habits, we have to step out in faith. Some Christians spend so much time in introspection that they fail to seize the initiative of aggressive faith. There's another side to the equation: "Let us run with endurance the race marked out for us." Once the load is lifted, we have to move out in pursuit of God's will. There are decisions to make, challenges to be tackled, obstacles to be surmounted. We don't have to go in our own strength, but we do have to go.

Here's the key: Once we cast aside the loads that keep us from reaching our spiritual potential, we have the stamina to hold up under life's tough demands. The strength comes as we "fix our eyes on Jesus, the author and perfecter of our faith" (Hebrews 12:2). Freed from the fatigue of sin and triviality, we keep a steadfast gaze on the overcoming power of Christ who "endured the cross" (12:2) as he kept his eyes on the Father's glorious purpose.

There's a race to run. Do your part, and watch God energize you to accomplish his will.

— • —

I never realized that my thoughts and habits can hinder my spiritual growth. Lord Jesus, help me to discover those areas that are roadblocks. Heal them so that their baggage will no longer weigh me down.

Touchstone

God is the ultimate
baggage handler.

If you falter in times of trouble, how small is your strength!

PROVERBS 24:10

Preparing for the Storms

---•---

The day will come. Or already has come. A sudden storm—it could be physical, financial, relational, spiritual—will strike. It may slam into us or someone we love.

It's okay if our knees buckle, our hearts race, or our anxiety levels rise. That's normal. But headlong adversity is no time to panic, flee, or faint. We must withstand the onslaught and put our face into the winds of adversity.

Don't misunderstand me. This is not about the survival of the fittest. We don't have to be spiritual superheroes to make it through the dark and stormy nights. In fact, God has designed a rather ordinary means to help us endure the tough times: We best survive the surges of suffering when we have spent ample time following God in the very practical rounds of life. If we wait until the "times of trouble" hit to be spiritually ready, we will be in for a difficult battle.

This elevates routine and repetition to new heights. For whatever reason, these terms are not very appealing to a culture that constantly seeks new thrills. I'm all for the excitement of something new—every photograph in this book called for a great sense of adventure—but absolutely nothing can replace the value of sticking to a daily schedule.

Great power lives in the mundane moments of life when we are practicing basic spiritual disciplines. Every day that we spend time with the Lord, delving into his Word, praying about matters that concern us, is strengthening our soul. We may not feel it. We may not see the benefits. If anything, we may sense a disconnect between the routine and the rewards, and abandon the exercises. This we do at great peril.

We may not be able to recall an exact spiritual promise when trouble breaks unexpectedly into our lives, but we have logged enough time in the Scriptures to know where to look. We may not know how to pray or what to ask, but we do know that God hears and answers the pleas of his people, especially in seasons of distress. You see, every time we read, study, pray, worship, fellowship, and obey God, we reinforce our spiritual armor. We encounter Christ, and he builds us up and readies us for the tempest ahead.

Remember what happened to Job? He was devastated—losing family, property, and wealth all in a matter of moments—yet he somehow managed to honor God with affirmations of trust. Read the first few verses of the first chapter. Job was an upright man (1:1) and made sure he offered appropriate sacrifices for his family (1:5). But here is the stickler: "This was Job's regular custom" (1: 5). Sure, Job had words with God over his loss, but he trusted in God's sovereignty in the end. This was possible because he had laid a solid foundation of obedience to Jehovah before the whirlwind of woe.

Never underestimate the value of the routine. If your heart is in the right place and you know that all we have is through God's grace, then you'll be prepared for the storm swell. And you will survive, for God has strengthened you.

Help me, Father, to hold in my heart all your many promises from your Word. Let your Word be the foundation that secures me during the storms of life.

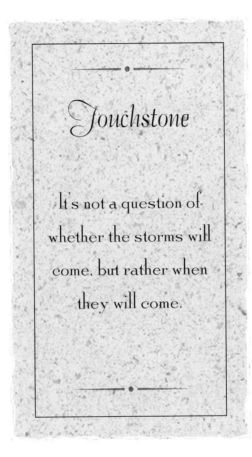

Touchstone

It's not a question of
whether the storms will
come, but rather when
they will come.

A friend loves at all times, and a brother is born for adversity.

PROVERBS 17:17

The Power of Friendship

Moses was a great leader, but he needed Aaron's rhetorical skills. David was a great escape artist, but Jonathan's help was vital when he was on the run from Saul. Paul spread the gospel far and wide, but not without the help of men like Barnabas, Luke, and Silas.

Godly friends are priceless. When we're down, they can pick us up. When we are scared, they can give us courage. When we're confused, they can share good counsel. Although the first person we should run to in time of need is Christ, the next best move we can make is to share our concern with a friend in Christ.

The kind of friend that can be a source of spiritual strength is a good listener. We've all probably encountered the person who loves to talk, but a real friend is someone who will hear us out. Often, the mere process of talking over our difficulties brings us to some conclusion or at least helps clear our thinking. The friend who listens is the person who genuinely cares for us.

The person who can be God's instrument of wisdom and refreshment is also one who will speak the truth to us, but not in a condemning fashion. "Faithful are the wounds of a friend" (Proverbs 27:6 NKJV). When godly friends notice sin in our lives, they know to help us face the problem without self-righteous smugness. They can help us spot erroneous thinking and steer us away from misguided assumptions.

A godly friend values the truth above all else. Perhaps our friendship has some built-in affinities—we both like to play golf, or visit a coffeehouse on weekends, or watch good movies. Still, the person of Christ, and thus the love for the truth, is at the center of the relationship. If a friend is willing to compromise the truth for the sake of friendship, then the relationship has lost its redemptive value. Nathan was no doubt a friend to David, but probably even more so after he spoke the painful truth about David's adulterous affair.

I enjoy friends who have a good sense of humor. A merry heart is like good medicine, the Bible says, and a friend who laughs is indispensable. There is healing power in laughter. While there is always the occasion for somberness, joviality is a keystone for a beneficial friendship.

Note that all the above qualities describe our Friend, Christ Jesus. The Lord listens patiently to our complaints, our praises, and our just plain chatter. He loves to hear our voice. He always speaks honestly, but gently, to our waywardness. Our fellowship with Christ is one of delightful friendship.

Develop Christ-centered friendships in which you can find renewal and give renewal, in which you can be strengthened in your faith and offer challenges, in which you can be loved and give love. Pray about them, cultivate them, ask the Lord to bless them. The knitting together of souls is divine tapestry of great worth and beauty.

———— ❖ ————

Dear Friend, I am so glad I can call you Friend. You are many things to me—Lord, Savior, Father. But in times of trouble, it's your friendship that carries me through.

Touchstone

What a friend we have
in Jesus!

My grace is sufficient for you, for my power is made perfect in weakness.

2 Corinthians 12:9

The Power of Weakness

—— ❧ ——

When we think about power in our culture, we typically associate images of wealth, authority, influence, privilege, and dominance. Rich athletes are powerful. Party leaders are powerful. Savvy businesspeople are powerful.

Would we ever say a support group for mothers of autistic children came together for a power lunch? Would we ever think a gathering of field missionaries from around the world could wield international influence?

From a cultural perspective, this is nonsense. But from a biblical perspective, it is quintessentially true. True power, the kind of strength that is the most enduring and admirable, comes from weakness. God, whose ways are higher and different than ours, has designated weakness and humility as the peculiar power base for genuine Christian living.

We think of the apostle Paul in lustrous terms, but his resumé in the Jewish culture took a decided dip once he followed Christ. What he boasted in before his salvation was an impressive pedigree that established him among the religious elite of his day (Philippians 3:1–6). His conversion to Christianity caused a radical shift.

"Therefore I will boast all the more gladly about my weaknesses, so that Christ's power may rest on me. That is why, for Christ's sake, I delight in weaknesses, in insults, in hardships, in persecutions, in difficulties. For when I am weak, then I am strong" (2 Corinthians 12:9–10).

The notion of power was completely stripped of any connection to cultural distinctions. Wealth and health can be lost overnight. A life built on the cultural definition of power can instantly crumble when those criteria are no longer met. Real power comes from the person of Jesus Christ. Real power, God's kind, shows up best in frail people.

Weakness is God's condition for power because weakened people are most dependent on Jesus Christ for strength. Problems knock out the artificial props of cultural power, but enhance the strength of people whose power rests on their relationship to Christ. The bigger the problem, the weaker we become, the more we find the mercy and help of Christ in our time of need.

Rather than rail against your frailty, celebrate it. Let it spur you to lean more heavily on Christ. You are weak, but Christ is strong.

———— • ————

Father, you are my strength. Help me to stop striving after artificial power or the power that the world tries to sell. Keep me focused on you and what you can do for me and through me when I remain yielded to you.

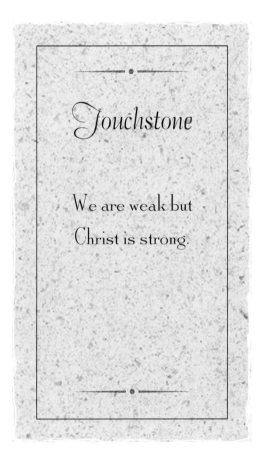

Touchstone

We are weak but
Christ is strong.

Do not be afraid. Stand firm and you will see the deliverance the LORD will bring you today.

EXODUS 14:13

Who's Fighting Your Battles?

We all must face obstacles that cannot be overcome apart from the Lord's supernatural assistance.

David, as a young man, came face to face with the giant Philistine warrior, Goliath. We all know the story, but can we recall the triumphant cry of David only moments before he rushed into combat? "For the battle is the LORD's, and he will give all of you into our hands" (1 Samuel 17:47), the shepherd with the sling shouted. And Goliath fell.

Jehoshaphat, king of Judah, was surrounded by fierce armies. Vastly outnumbered, Jehoshaphat turned his attention to the Lord in a public fast and heard this prophecy uttered: "Do not be afraid or discouraged because of this vast army. For the battle is not yours, but God's" (2 Chronicles 20:15). God so routed the enemy that it took several days for the men of Judah to carry away the spoils of victory.

When King Hezekiah faced a siege from an Assyrian army, he encouraged his leaders, as they worked to fortify Jerusalem, with these words: "With him [the opposing king] is only the arm of flesh, but with us is the LORD our God to help us and to fight our battles" (2 Chronicles 32:8).

Confronted with problems that could not be overcome by human tenacity or wisdom, these men learned the marvelous truth that every Christian can know: *God himself fights our battles for us* (Exodus 14:13). God is with us, indwelling us through his Holy Spirit, to help us in our times of desperation. The difficulties we face may seem insurmountable, but God can do the impossible.

God fights our battles because what assails us also assails him. David knew that Goliath was fighting against Jehovah God himself when he derided the armies of Israel. The person who walks in intimate fellowship with Christ can rightly invoke God's supernatural help in distressing times. God will not be mocked by the forces of evil that seek to harm the believer, and he will move heaven and earth to exalt his name in our lives. We are the apple of God's eye, and he will protect his children.

God is faithful to come to our aid when we cry out to him. Jehoshaphat pleaded before the Almighty God, and the Lord responded with a miraculous deliverance. As we commit our seemingly intractable problems to Christ, we shift the burden for a solution from our shoulders to his. The problems we face become a battleground for prevailing prayer. God is the one who must work, and prayer is the prime mover.

God fights our battles because he is the Sovereign Lord of all. Hezekiah knew the enemy, though clearly superior in numbers, was no match for God. Whatever our problems may be, as big and imposing and frightening as they are, they are not equal to the matchless might of a God for whom nothing is impossible. God truly is bigger than any problem we face.

Count on God's help today. You may be tired, but God never grows weary. You may have failed repeatedly in your efforts, but God will never fail you. Trust that the formidable enemy you face is no match for the awesome God you serve.

What a relief to know that you are for me and you really want to handle my problems. I lay my burdens at your feet and rest, knowing you are fighting my battles and protecting me along the way.

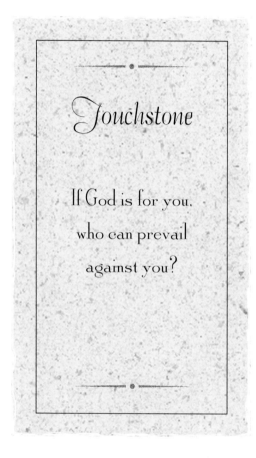

Touchstone

If God is for you,

who can prevail

against you?

You need to persevere so that when you have done
the will of God, you will receive what he has promised.

HEBREWS 10:36

Hanging In There

What a thrill to know we can be "strengthened with all power according to his glorious might" (Colossians 1:11). We all stand in need of God's power. But what does God give us strength for? The answer, found in the second portion of this verse, may be a bit surprising.

God gives his power so that we may possess "great endurance and patience." God isn't necessarily sustaining us so that we might enjoy bliss and personal fulfillment (though he often does grant us these blessings). He does not empower us to simply make our agenda happen without a hitch. God fortifies our spirits so that we might have the stamina it takes to successfully complete the Christian journey.

Trials and temptation do come our way—almost every day. The spiritual quality of endurance is a necessity if we are to keep moving forward while confronting obstacles.

The apostle James actually said we should be quite pleased when troubles abound. "Consider it pure joy, my brothers, whenever you face trials of many kinds" (James 1:2). Is that some kind of warped spiritual thinking? Who really thinks that worries and difficulties should be occasions for rapture?

God has his reasons. "Because you know that the testing of your faith develops perseverance" (James 1:3). Afflictions have a purpose: to cultivate endurance. Often, believers who haven't been thoroughly tested by trials are not much help to other believers, nor do they usually have the right spiritual stuff for the long haul. They are like the seeds cast on the ground that sprout and die quickly.

Endurance leads to something greater. "Perseverance must finish its work so that you may be mature and complete, not lacking anything" (James 1:4). The more we hang in there when the world is shaking around us, the deeper our level of faith and fellowship with Christ becomes. Mature Christians are not perfect people; they are faithful men and women who, by the strength Christ gives, haven't given up in adversity.

Think about the progression. God gives us strength. That strength is so we might develop spiritual endurance as we face life's trials. The endurance we gain helps us make spiritual progress, moving forward in our prayer life, our devotional life, our service to Christ and other people, our worship—every facet of the Christian experience.

God knows we have many challenges ahead. He knows we need his strength to advance through our adversity. He willingly and generously provides his power to help us endure the rough road ahead.

"Run with perseverance the race" (Hebrews 12:1) so that you might have the joy of having run and finished well.

———— ❖ ————

You are so great and mighty, Lord. I want to praise you for the strength you provide for me to run the race of life. You are with me all along the way, and you are there at the finish line to welcome me home.

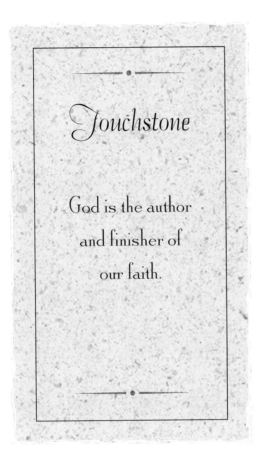

Touchstone

God is the author
and finisher of
our faith.

Who am I, O Sovereign LORD, and what is my family,
that you have brought me this far?

2 SAMUEL 7:18

Strength to Give

David was ecstatic in his praise. God had chosen his son Solomon to build the temple, and David, realizing God's blessings on his life, lifted his heart to the heavens.

"Yours, O LORD, is the kingdom; you are exalted as head over all. Wealth and honor come from you; you are the ruler of all things. In your hands are strength and power to exalt and give strength to all" (1 Chronicles 29:11–12). What a majestic proclamation from a man after God's own heart!

David, the mighty warrior, skilled king, and gifted writer, knew the source of real strength. It begins and ends with God himself. Far above all the fame and fortune that David had and infinitely beyond all the treasures of earth is the person of Jehovah God.

The once shepherd boy, the rawest and youngest of his father's clan, could look at the end of his rich and stormy life and see the hand of a sovereign God at work. What else could account for his giant-slaying feat, rise to leadership, and spiritual intimacy with the Lord but the hand of God? Others could have been chosen; but David relied on the Lord for his help, and so God's strength led him to victory and consoled him in adversity. When David hid from Saul in dark, damp caves, shivering in cold desert nights, God sustained him. When David led men into battle against superior odds, God gave him victory.

The same strength that God gave David can be ours too. We may not become rulers or poets or statespeople, but God will give us the strength we need for the tasks he has assigned us. All we need to do, like David, is believe and receive.

Paul said, "I pray also that the eyes of your heart may be enlightened in order that you may know the hope to which he has called you, the riches of his glorious inheritance in the saints, and his incomparably great power for us who believe" (Ephesians 1:18–19). When we believe in Christ as our Savior from the penalty of sin, we are strengthened with the very life of Christ. When we believe in his power to deliver us from the stronghold of sin's dominion, we receive his overcoming power.

Strength and power are in God's hands; and his hands are not clenched tightly to withhold his blessings but opened wide to give us his strength. As a teenager, David knew that he must put his trust in an awesome God and receive victory that only God could give. Others looked to their armies, their wealth, and their abundant resources for strength. But David, with childlike faith, received power from the Sovereign God who alone could impart it. We are no different. God provides the strength we need. For work. For home. For battles. For giants. For conquests we could never have dreamed about. Power is his to give and ours to receive by pure and simple faith. "Thanks be to God! He gives us the victory through our Lord Jesus Christ" (1 Corinthians 15:57).

Don't depend on yourself to find strength. Ask God to let you rest in his.

Heavenly Father, when I read how a great and mighty king like David depended completely upon you, it humbles me so that I, too, depend solely on you for my strength for each day. Thank you for David and for the love and dependence he demonstrated.

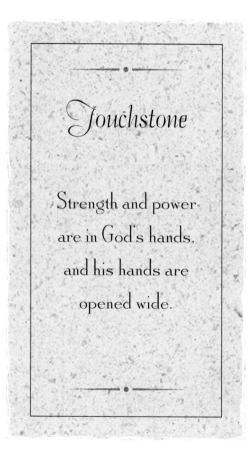

Touchstone

Strength and power
are in God's hands,
and his hands are
opened wide.

I can do everything through him who gives me strength.

God Can

I can't, but Christ can." In this small statement lies the secret to dealing with the struggles of life, whatever their cause or nature. We don't have all the resources to handle the problem—nor all the answers—even when we think we might. But God certainly does.

In a sense, this is very liberating. We don't have to constantly engineer our own solutions. We have a responsibility to do all we can and learn all we can, but the key to success lies in Christ's strength in us, not our own power.

The Holy Spirit, whom we received at salvation, is the very power of Christ in us. He lives in us to help us do the works of God by the power of God. He helps us experience the very life of Christ. When Paul said he could do all things through the person of Christ, he was touting God's sufficiency, not his. He was pointing us to the adequacy of Christ, the superabundant power that is available to every believer.

But what does it mean to do all things through Christ, to confess that we can't, but that he can through us? We experience the life of Christ as we learn to abide in him. Paul had learned the secret to contentment in all circumstances (Philippians 4:11–12): abiding in Christ. "I am the vine; you are the branches. If a man remains in me and I in him, he will bear much fruit; apart from me you can do nothing" (John 15:5).

Abiding in Christ is simply realizing that Christ is our life and that he alone supplies all our needs. Abiding in Jesus is counting on God to give us all the strength we need, all the guidance we seek, all the love we desperately want. Abiding is not some sort of mystical experience but daily obedience to the Word of God and supreme trust in the Lord's supply. As a branch draws all its life and fruit from the vine, so we draw all we need from the Vine, Jesus Christ. Whether it's love, joy, peace, patience, kindness, or anything else we need to tackle our obstacles, we can receive it from Christ who gives us strength.

We must confess the truth of Scripture: "Apart from me you can do nothing." That doesn't mean we shouldn't do anything, but that everything we do is dependent on Christ's enabling.

With God's help, all things are possible; without God's help, nothing is. You can't, and that's okay; but Christ can, and that's fantastic.

———— ● ————

I want to live my life through you, Lord Jesus. Show me how to abide in you, as a branch clings to its vine. Teach me how to view everything that touches my life as coming through you first.

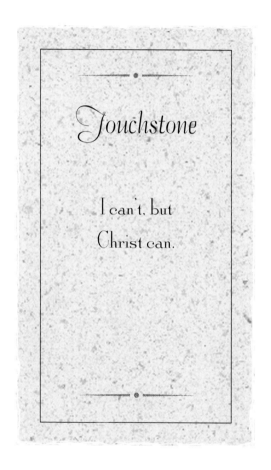

Touchstone

I can't, but
Christ can.

You will keep in perfect peace him whose mind is steadfast, because he trusts in you.

ISAIAH 26:3

Don't Worry, Trust God

Worry and fear sap strength as few other emotions do. When we are anxious, fretful, or afraid, our ability to handle tough situations is severely compromised. These emotions slowly drain our strength and faith with their extraordinarily negative pull, leaving us feeling progressively helpless and vulnerable.

The battle to trust God and gain his power is largely in the mind. Runaway emotions can mount serious assaults on our confidence in God. Our adversary, the devil, knows that if he can keep our minds hostage to doubt and unbelief, the awareness of God's strength and confidence in his power to deliver are sorely diminished.

When fears and worries come in like a flood, the first line of defense is an honest admission of our apprehension. David often wrestled with great fears. He didn't try to suppress them, to bury them, but took them right to the Lord. "When I am afraid, I will trust in you" (Psalm 56:3). David did not say *if* I am afraid, but *when* I am afraid. David readily confessed his worries and did not hide them from the Lord. Admitting his fears, he turned his attention to trust in God. When anxious, we can tell God about it. He knows anyway, and acknowledging our fears to him is the initial step to replacing them with trust. But we cannot stop there. Confessing our fears, we must come to God in prayer and thanksgiving. "Do not be anxious about anything, but in everything, by prayer and petition, with thanksgiving, present your requests to God" (Philippians 4:6). Prayer, laden with thanksgiving, is where the battle is fought and won against worry and fear.

When we pray earnestly and boldly to the Lord regarding our concerns, we are taking them to Almighty God, whose power and love are more than adequate to surmount our worries. Our prayer focuses on the sufficiency of God (Is there anything he can't handle?), and our praise exalts his greatness. The greater we see the power of the Lord ready to work in our circumstances, the weaker fear's hold will be on us. God has gripped our lives with his grace and pledges to help in our time of need (Hebrews 4:16). Fears may seek to unnerve and destabilize us. But if we magnify the presence and power of God, they will not overwhelm us—for God is with us, for us, in us, and on our side. Nothing can match his wisdom or strength.

The incredible truth about fear that few people recognize is that when we allow it to drive us into the grace and mercy of God, it can serve to grow our faith, not destroy it. When we learn to pray and trust about everything and worry about nothing, our fears become our allies. They only make us stronger in Christ, not weaker, because we learn to rush into the arms of the Savior who stills our anxieties with his peace.

God works everything together for good (Romans 8:28), and he can use even your most alarming emotions to infuse your mind and heart with his power. Let the peace of God guard your heart. Begin to fix your mind on the good and noble things of God (Philippians 4:7–8) by bringing your fears to Christ and affirming his power and greatness.

———— • ————

I lay at your feet, Mighty Father, and present my afflictions to you with open hands. I am releasing the fears that have come with them and resting in your loving arms as you assume responsibility for the outcome.

Touchstone

God is in control.

Blessed is he who is kind to the needy.

PROVERBS 14:21

Contagious Strength

We each experience pleasant seasons in our lives when all is well. God has blessed us with health, our relationship with him is thriving, and our circumstances are favorable. Especially in these times when our physical, emotional, and spiritual stamina is in peak condition, we need to remember to help those who are struggling.

The Lord uses our own trials to forge the kind of genuine compassion we can lovingly extend to others caught in the throes of similar dilemmas (2 Corinthians 1:3–4). God gives us the opportunity and responsibility to reach out and help the unfortunate and distressed.

Paul wrote to the church at Rome, "We who are strong ought to bear with the failings of the weak and not to please ourselves. Each of us should please his neighbor for his good, to build him up" (Romans 15:1–2).

The strength we have now is not merely for our personal enjoyment; it is also for picking up other brothers or sisters in Christ who are wounded and troubled. We don't have to look far to find people in need. They probably sit next to us at the office, live in our neighborhoods, or occupy the same pews with us at church.

Someone insightfully remarked that humankind is "one vast need." God can use our simple acts of kindness and words of encouragement to lift up a broken and bowed soul just as surely as he has worked through others to minister to us in our times of need.

Rather than concentrating on pleasing ourselves, we should help bear the burdens of the helpless and look for positive and practical ways to bring healing, relief, and rejuvenation. In so doing, we act like our Father in heaven who stoops down to make us great, defends the widow and the orphan, and moves heaven and earth to respond to our cries for help. Prophetically speaking of Christ, Isaiah wrote, "A bruised reed he will not break, and a smoldering wick he will not snuff out" (Isaiah 42:3). God, Father of the fatherless and Mender of broken hearts, seeks to gently restore the faltering and hopeless. Such compassion should mark us as his sons and daughters.

You who are strong, help the weak. "Blessed is he who has regard for the weak; the LORD delivers him in times of trouble. The LORD will protect him and preserve his life" (Psalm 41:1–2).

Can you think of someone now who is at the point of exhaustion? A worried mother? An anxious father? A hurt child? A discouraged teenager? This person needs God's touch. With the strength God has given you, take time to pray, asking the Lord how you can come to his or her aid. It doesn't take much. Maybe a phone call. Maybe a visit. Maybe a lunch. God knows, and his power can flow through you to revive the fainthearted.

Precious Lord, bring to my mind someone I can minister to. Soften my heart to be more aware of the hurts and needs of others. Strengthen me in knowledge as I seek to spread your contagious love and power.

Touchstone

God's power grows
as it is shared.

Blessed are those whose strength is in you, who have
set their hearts on pilgrimage.

PSALM 84:5

The Great Destination

There is great power in destination. A family headed home for the holidays zips merrily through hundreds of miles that might otherwise seem monotonous. A young person en route to a first job navigates the winding highways with great expectations. A runner with the finish line in sight ignores the ache and picks up the pace to break the tape.

I sometimes wonder if we realize how great is the power of the Christian's ultimate destination—eternity in the presence of Jesus Christ. Heaven is where every Christian will one day lodge in perpetual delight, our home, the most joyful place we will ever know.

But if you are like me, the promise of heaven seems awfully distant, residing in a land of biblical metaphors. We do not dispute its reality or ecstasy, but we often have only glimpses of this truth as we go through the gritty demands of life. After all, heaven is so perfect, and we are so imperfect.

The writer of the eighty-fourth psalm gives us some help for how our longing for God and his reality can empower us for the journey. Yearning for the beauty of worship in God's house in Zion (Jerusalem), the wandering Korahite is refreshed as he affirms that God is with him in his exile.

He may not physically be in the temple, but his heart is set on the pilgrimage. The power of the destination, the allure of heaven, isn't the arrival; understanding is where the journey leads, whatever the circumstances. There is purpose and meaning even in the confusing twists and turns of life on earth when they lead us to intimacy with Christ.

When our hearts are set on seeking God, when our souls are bent toward loving God, we can even go through painful places and somehow bring to them the very genuine touch of Christ. When our hearts are focused on knowing God and we refuse to be detoured by the appeal or disillusionment of surroundings, we inexplicably gain strength. I have seen people in the midst of problems who impart courage to others, who find fellowship with Christ strangely sweet in bitter places. In a very authentic sense, heaven does come down as Christ's presence is acknowledged through personal trust and worship. The highway to heaven runs through many valleys.

The displaced Korahite also affirmed the power of a safe landing. "Each appears before God in Zion" (84:7). Heaven is a sure thing for the believer in Christ. The longing for God we have in this life will be consummated when we meet Christ face-to-face. God has guaranteed adoption into his family through the sacrifice of his Son for our sins. This is God's promise and provision.

The journey is arduous, but God is with you. Hold on to the promise that your destination is secure and that God awaits you.

———— • ————

No matter what I'm going through, I'm so comforted in knowing that my final journey is to you, dear Lord. It's one thing I know I can count on. You love me more than I can fathom; you sent your Son to die for me so I may one day be with you.

Touchstone

For the believer,
all roads lead
to heaven.

Experience God's Touch . . .

. . . with help from the popular devotional books in Charles Stanley's A Touch of His . . . series. Each book contains thirty-one meditations on a particular theme by Dr. Stanley, along with a Scripture passage, a personal prayer, and a "Touchstone," or personal application. In addition, each meditation is accompanied by beautiful original photography by Dr. Stanley himself, which makes these books perfect for gift-giving as well as personal reading.

Pick up your copies of these inspirational books at your favorite Christian bookstore.

A Touch of His Goodness:
Meditations on God's
Abundant Goodness
Hardcover 0-310-21489-0

A Touch of His Freedom:
Meditations on Freedom
in Christ
Hardcover 0-310-54620-6

A Touch of His Love:
Meditations on Knowing and
Receiving the Love of God
Hardcover 0-310-54560-9
Audio pages 0-310-54569-2

A Touch of His Peace:
Meditations on Experiencing
the Peace of God
Hardcover 0-310-54550-1
Audio pages 0-310-54558-7

A Touch of His Power:
Meditations on God's
Awesome Power
Hardcover 0-310-21492-0

A Touch of His Wisdom:
Meditations on the Book
of Proverbs
Hardcover 0-310-54540-4

The Blessings of Brokenness:
Why God Allows Us to Go Through Hard Times

No matter how great your faith in God, pain and grief are a part of life.

Perhaps you've already experienced circumstances so shattering you may wonder today whether it's even possible to pick up the pieces. And maybe you can't. But God can—and the good news is, he wants to reassemble the shards of your life into a wholeness that only the broken can know.

With gentle wisdom, Dr. Stanley shines light on the process of being broken. He reveals the ways we protest against it. And he gives us an inspiring look beyond the pain to the promise of blessing.

"Brokenness is what God uses to replace our self-life with his desires and intents for us," says Stanley. Its end is blessing far greater than we could ever discover apart from being broken: spiritual maturity and joyous intimacy with God; greater depth and power in our ministry to others; new dimensions of freedom, strength, and peace. And a wholeness that comes as God himself reassembles us into someone more closely resembling Jesus Christ.

Hardcover 0-310-20026-1
Audio pages 0-310-29421-6

CHARLES STANLEY

THE BLESSINGS

OF BROKENNESS

WHY GOD ALLOWS US TO GO
THROUGH HARD TIMES

We want to hear from you. Please send your comments about this book to us in care of the address below. Thank you.

ZondervanPublishingHouse
Grand Rapids, Michigan 49530
http://www.zondervan.com